The Care and Breeding of the African Spurred Tortoise
Geochelone sulcata

By
Richard and Robyn Wilson

Carapace Press
London

1997

ACKNOWLEDGMENTS

We would like to say thank you to all the people that were so gracious with their time and advice in helping us put this book together.

Kevin and Sue Hanley: Thank you for your undivided attention and patience with much needed help and advice in the world of computers, which had a great deal to do with this book, and for your expertise in photography, we could not have done it without you.

Christian Ginkel: I would like to give special thanks to Chris. He has been a very good friend of ours for many years, and has extensive knowledge in keeping and breeding tortoises. He has always been just a phone call away and willing to help in any way.

Chuck Vincent: We would like to say thank you, Chuck, for your many hours of help and advice. Your extensive knowledge in keeping and breeding tortoises has been a great help to us.

Photographs copyright Kevin and Sue Hanley

All rights reserved. No part of this publication may be copied in any form without the prior written consent of the publishers.

First Edition, 1997
Printed by ProPrint, Carmarthen, Wales, U.K.

Published by:
Carapace Press
BM Tortoise
London
WC1N 3XX
England

International Tel/Fax 44 - (1267) - 211578
E-mail sales-dept@vidi-herp.com http://www.vidi-herp.com

ISBN 1 873943 51 2

Table of Contents

Introduction	5
General information	7
Distribution	8
Choosing a healthy tortoise	9
Outdoor enclosures	11
Diet and nutrition	13
How to sex tortoises	19
Breeding *Geochelone sulcata*	21
Eggs and incubation	22
Veterinary problems	27
Frequently asked questions	31

Care and Breeding of the African Spurred Tortoise

Kevin and Sue Hanley

INTRODUCTION

Our fascination with tortoises started about 12 years ago when we saw our first desert tortoise hatchling. It was without a doubt the most fascinating animal we had ever encountered. After several attempts at begging, the breeder of these tortoises finally agreed to give up two of his hatchlings. We immediately took them home, set them up in an aquarium, and proceeded to get as much information on these reptiles as possible. That proved to be virtually impossible, as no matter how hard we looked or who we talked to there was very little information available. After many months of frustration we finally found a few experienced tortoise keepers and thanks to their help put an end to our frustration. Today there are many very successful tortoise breeders and herpetological clubs dedicated to keeping and breeding reptiles. These individuals and clubs have proved to be invaluable to the tortoise enthusiast. Many private breeders are willing to share their methods of success, and most clubs have open meetings, publish newsletters, and have many guest speakers on all areas of reptile keeping.

We now breed several types of tortoises including the African spurred tortoise or *Geochelone sulcata*. This book was inspired by hundreds of phone calls from people seeking information on the proper care of their newly acquired pet. Combining our personal experience along with reading everything we could find on sulcatas, it is our hope to help the novice tortoise keeper get the information needed to successfully care for and eventually breed the sulcata. We believe that through captive breeding someday the importation of many thousands of tortoises per year will finally cease. Wild populations of all species of tortoise are decreasing at an alarming rate due to habitat destruction and collecting for the pet trade. A very high percentage of imported tortoises die within their first year of captivity due to improper care. With tortoises becoming more popular every year, there are many scientific and private studies being carried out today. With these studies comes a wealth of new information on habitats, husbandry, and general care of these captivating reptiles. It is up to the private breeder and other breeding facilities to meet the growing demand for tortoises, by supplying healthy captive-bred stock, and most important of all by providing the information needed to successfully maintain these animals. We welcome any comments or suggestions you may have about the contents of this book. Like many other people we are still learning.

Please send any comments or suggestions to:
Desert Reptiles c/o Richard or Robyn Wilson
P.O.Box 10314
Glendale, Arizona 85318
e-mail: rdww@paloverde.com

Identification of shell plates (scutes)

Top (Carapace)

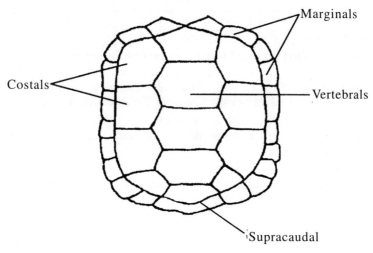

Bottom (Plastron)

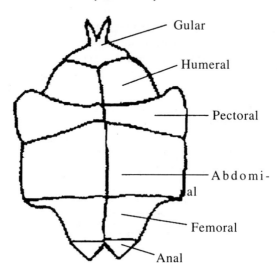

GENERAL INFORMATION

Geochelone sulcata, commonly named the African Spurred Tortoise, is frequently also referred to, in error, as the Spur-thighed Tortoise. This latter is a Mediterranean origin tortoise belonging to the genus *Testudo*, and is a creature with very different requirements. It only attains a fraction of the size of a sulcata, so be certain to avoid this confusion when choosing your tortoise. The name 'Spurred Tortoise' comes from the two or three large 'spurs' located on each side of the tail. The sulcata is the largest mainland tortoise, smaller only than the Galapagos and Aldabra island giant tortoises. Adults can attain 33 inches in length with weights of up to 200 pounds. The sulcata is a very heavily built tortoise, with large powerful legs covered with thick heavy scales. The skin color is usually straw colored or yellow. It has a wide and flattened carapace, containing 5 vertebral scutes, 4 coastal scutes and 11 marginal scutes. The supracaudal scute is undivided with the nuchal scute being absent. The anterior marginals are strongly reverted in larger males. The carapace color can range from dark brown to a light tan, or yellow. The plastron is usually straw colored or yellow with forked gulars, very narrow pectoral scutes, and anal scutes deeply notched. The males have a deep plastral cavity and as adults are larger than females.

Geochelone sulcata is native to sub-Saharan Africa, inhabiting dry desert areas along the southern border of the Sahara desert from Mauritania to Ethiopia. In recent years they have been exported from Africa in large numbers to many other parts of the world for the pet trade. In captivity sulcatas prove to be very adaptable and hardy if given the proper diet and housing. They have have often been referred to as the dogs of the tortoises world. Having a very curious nature and bold personality, they are docile and easily tamed, adapting to captivity with seemingly little effort. Availability, adaptability, and personality has made *Geochelone sulcata* one of the most popular tortoises with both beginner and advanced tortoise enthusiasts.

DISTRIBUTION

The African Spurred tortoise (*Geochelone sulcata*) is located in central Africa. Inhabiting dry arid deserts from the west coast of Senegal and Mauritania, east to southern and central Mali, southern Niger, northern Nigeria, central and eastern Chad, central and eastern Sudan, and central to northern Ethiopia.

Temperature and annual rainfall in various areas where *Geochelone sulcata* is found.

	High	Low	Annual rainfall	'Wet' season
Senegal	86°	63°	8-12 inches	July - September
Mauritania	95°	55°	2-4 inches	August
Mali	109°	56°	4-8 inches	July - August
Niger	106°	59°	4-8 inches	September - October
Chad	106°	58°	4-12 inches	June - August
Sudan	104°	50°	4-8 inches	July - August
Ethiopia	104°	55°	2-4 inches	July - September

It should be noted that the figures given for rainfall are subject to considerable variation. Prolonged periods of drought are typical throughout this region, and in some years, only a fraction of an inch may fall. When this happens, tortoises, along with many other reptiles, may estivate for many months on end. The temperatures given here are the closest major settlements to known *Geochelone sulcata* populations.

CHOOSING A HEALTHY TORTOISE

There are several things to look for when choosing a tortoise:

❑ Sulcatas are very large and heavily built tortoises. When choosing your tortoise, make sure the animal feels heavy for its size. Pick it up to make sure.

❑ The eyes should be full and clear. By full, we mean not sunken into the head. Look for any discharge from the eyes. When the weather is very hot they will often have a clear discharge from their eyes, however, no white or milky discharge should be visible. Sulcatas have very good eyesight so they should appear very active and alert.

❑ The nose should be dry and clear of any discharge. Listen to the animal breathe; there should be no wheezing or coughing. Breathing involves expanding and contracting the throat. If the tortoise is breathing hard or using the front legs to pump air in and out of its lungs the animal should be avoided. These symptoms are sometimes early signs of respiratory problems, such as pneumonia. Note that this behaviour can be associated with stress, however, and that handling or overheating may induce these symptoms in a perfectly healthy animal.

❑ The carapace and plastron should be free of cracks and peeling. Small chips and abrasions are usually not a problem. Look the animal over thoroughly, checking the plastron and the carapace.

❑ The skin should be without any recent injuries, parasites, or sores.

❑ When purchasing your sulcata get as much information about the animal as possible, such as which types of foods have been fed on a regular basis. This can be a problem if the tortoise was fed on high protein diets such as dog or cat foods. Has the animal been housed with other types of tortoises? If so, viral and bacterial problems may be encountered.

❑ Always keep any new arrivals out of your enclosures until they have been quarantined for at least 30 days or longer. 90 days is even better. New animals could have viral or bacterial infections that you are not aware of. Introducing the animal to other animals can lead to major problems and disappointments by infecting your entire collection. Under no circumstances should tortoises of different species be housed in the same enclosures. Tortoises from different parts of the world can carry pathogens that are common and natural to one animal's system, but if transmitted to other types of tortoises they can be deadly.

A typical outdoor pen with heated tortoise house for use in cold weather. This type of pen is suitable for use with most large species, including Leopard, Aldabra and Sulcata tortoises.

Geochelone sulcata are extremely enthusiastic excavators. All pens must be carefully designed to prevent escape and should be monitored regularly.

OUTDOOR ENCLOSURES

Geochelone sulcata generally does best when housed outdoors, provided , that is, they are large enough to avoid predatory animals and birds and that the climate is suitable. Tortoises under 4 inches in length are best left indoors unless they are carefully watched and in an escape proof enclosure. Once your tortoises have reached 4 to 6 inches in length you might want to consider putting them in a well designed outdoor enclosure.

When you are designing your outdoor enclosure, always keep in mind that your tortoises are going to get very large so they need as much space as possible. Plant the area heavily with grasses and other foods for them to browse on. A two foot high wall seems to contain them with no problem of the animal escaping. All corners should have a plate of wood or metal across the top edge. Tortoises seem to have 'thing' for corners and climbing them is usually done with little effort.

Pen walls should be buried into the ground 4 to 6 inches, leaving 18 inches above ground, and made fromwood or other solid material so that the tortoises cannot see through them. Chain link or wire should be avoided. The tortoises can become caught in the wire, and being able to see through they never seem to settle down. They will pace constantly trying to find a way out. Solid walls will generally eliminate these problems.

Carefully plan for plants and trees in your enclosure, keeping the plants well out of reach of the tortoises or they will not last long. Toxic plants must be carefully avoided. Trees are needed for shade, and plants of various types are useful in supplying additional food. Putting shrubs and bushes in large planter barrels, such as whiskey barrels, works well and protects those plants you wish to avoid being eaten. Ensure that all planters are sufficiently large so that the tortoise cannot push them over.

It is very important to build a house for your tortoises to stay in during the winter months. Remember that these are very large animals. You need to make sure that any houses are large enough contain them for several days or even weeks. Our climate here in southern Arizona is very mild in winter compared to other areas, so our tortoise houses are not insulated .Yours may need to be insulated if you live in an area that receives snow or cold rains. In areas that receive snow your tortoises must remain indoors or be provided with a large outdoor heated house.

Our own tortoise houses measure 8 feet square and 4 feet high, and are made from 5/8 exterior plywood on a 2 by 4 frame. The roof is pitched so that it does not hold water or snow. Snow is very heavy and could collapse the roof of your tortoise house if it is insufficiently strong. The door is 4 feet square and is large enough to let the tortoises in and out, and is very nice for cleaning. Cleanliness is very important. Your tortoise house will need to be cleaned regularly.

Heat can be provided many different ways. Heat lamps and oil filled radiating electric heaters are the most popular. We use the electric oil filled heaters suspended from the roof so the tortoises cannot come into contact with them. Whatever method you use, take extreme care to avoid any risk of fire. Large tortoises can easily knock heaters over, with potentially fatal consequences. In very cold climates you may need to introduce floor heat along with heat from above. Sulcatas are thickly built tortoises and in some cases radiating heat from above may be insufficient to keep them from chilling. The floor of the house can be dirt or plywood. We use dirt because it is easy to clean. Whether you use dirt or wood, one of the many types of fiberglass pig blankets work very well for supplying floor heat. They are very durable even with large tortoises. The floor should also be designed so that the tortoises can not dig out. We use chainlink in the floor fastened to the bottom of the walls all the way around. Then about 12 inches of dirt is put on the floor to cover the chainlink. This allows the tortoises to dig in a little but they can't dig right out. Straw can also be used on the floor to give the tortoises more insulation during cold weather.

We do not recommend putting ponds or water holes in the enclosure. Standing water is very difficult to keep clean. It also provides a place for bacteria to flourish. Some large specimens will, however, drink from a dog's bowl.

Nutritional analysis of typical natural foods

Item	% protein	% fibre	% dry matter	% fat	% Ca	% P
Grass (winter)	4.00	37.00	40.00	1.00	0.75	0.06
Grass (summer)	6.00	n/a	n/a	2.00	0.35	0.20
Grass (lawn)	3.00	12.00	35.00	1.30	0.10	0.09
Forbs	9.00	n/a	n/a	2.75	1.80	0.40
Brome	8.50	31.00	35.00	1.00	0.28	0.23
Threeawn	6.30	35.00	n/a	1.50	0.60	0.09
Clover hay	11.00	30.00	n/a	1.90	1.00	0.20

Contents vary seasonally.

DIET AND NUTRITION

Sulcatas are very big eaters, to put it mildly. They will try to eat just about anything in their path and if they like it (which they probably will), then look out, they will eat it down to a nub. Check with your local plant nursery to make sure whatever plants that your tortoise will come in contact with are not poisonous. Sulcatas will eat almost anything they can get to, good or bad, poisonous or not.

FIBER

Fiber is one of the most important parts of the sulcata's diet, therefore grasses, leaves, vetches, alfalfa, and hays should make up the bulk of their diet. A diet low in fiber, as is the case with most store bought produce, is sure to cause digestive problems. Loose stools, colic, and poor health are just a few problems encountered when feeding your tortoise mainly store-bought produce.

Most, if not all, tortoise foods sold by pet dealers, are for the most part grossly inadequate for the sulcata's diet. Most are very high in proteins and fat, with fiber being very low and in some cases not present at all. These foods should be avoided! You can supply your sulcata with a very high fiber diet right in your own yard and save a lot of money in the process. Grow several types of grasses, vetches, hay, and many other types of natural foods right in the tortoises enclosure. Prickly pear cactus and other types of plants you don't want eaten to the ground should be planted outside the enclosure. If planted inside the enclosure put the plants in large planters so the tortoises cannot get to the plants or they will only last a few minutes. Large tortoises have an enormous appetite. Provided you do not use any fertilizers, or pesticides, you can also give grass clippings from other parts of your yard to your sulcatas. This helps with cleanup while supplying your tortoises with plenty of good quality high fiber food.

NATURAL FOODS

- ❑ Bales of hay, alfalfa, vetches, clovers, and grasses
- ❑ Opuntia ssp. Prickly Pear cactus and the fruits
- ❑ Leaves from trees such as Mulberry and Fig
- ❑ Flowers such as Rose, Dandelion and Hibiscus

Seeds can also be planted to help keep the enclosure from becoming over grazed. Plant many types of grasses, thistle, alfalfa, winter horse pasture mix, vetch, and clovers. The seeds should be planted in a closed off area from the tortoises. Sprouting seeds do not provide the sulcata with the nutrition needed, only after the plant has begun to establish itself should it be offered to the tortoise.

Examples of seeds that are suitable for cultivation as fodder include:

- Indian Wheat (*Plantago insularus*)
- Purple Three Awn *(Aristida purpurea)*
- Buffalograss *(Buchloe dactyloides)*
- Indian Rice Grass *(Oryzopsis hymenoides)*

Also try: Bermuda grass, Sahara, White Dutch Clover, Dichondra, Red Crimson-Inoculated Clover, White New Zealand-Raw Clover, Vetch Lana Raw, Vetch Purple Raw. These are just a few examples of the home-grown quality foods you can offer your sulcata on a daily basis.

FRESH PRODUCE

A sulcata's staple diet should not consist entirely of commercial produce. In the wild there is no such produce, only grass, leaves, and flowers. If you feel it necessary to feed your tortoise store-bought foods then here are some guide lines to go by.

The best foods to choose are those with a high calcium vs. low phosphorus ratio as well as being high in fiber. The calcium to phosphorus ratio should be two to one at a minimum, four or five parts calcium to one part phosphorus is best. Leafy greens are as high in fiber as you can get with fresh produce, but are still lacking in the amount of fiber necessary to keeping a tortoise healthy. Some of the better produce includes:

Mustard greens, turnip greens, romaine lettuce, parsley, carrot tops, cabbage, bell pepper, collard greens, kale, Brussels sprouts, yellow squash, and green onion. We suggest you only use commercial produce as an occasional supplement, no more than once a week.

OXALIC ACID

Oxalic acid is present in several foods that at first appear ideal for feeding to tortoises because of the high vitamin content or their high calcium to phosphorus ratio. Oxalic acid interferes with the absorption of calcium into the tortoises system, therefore, these foods should be avoided or used very seldom. Large amounts of oxalic acid are found in, rhubarb, spinach, and in Swiss chard.

PROTEIN & FAT

Geochelone sulcata are herbivores which means they are plant eaters. We do not recommend feeding your sulcatas animal proteins of any kind. This includes all dog food (canned or dry) or any other product containing animal proteins or fats.

High animal protein levels can cause serious problems in the long term maintenance of tortoises. It has been noted that excessive amounts of protein

NUTRITIONAL ANALYSIS OF COMMON SUBSTITUTE (CAPTIVE) FOODS

All figures are approximate averages in grams per 100g

Item	Protein	Fibre	Fat	Ca *	P*	Vit-A (IU)	
Apple	0.20	1.00	0.60	7.00	10.00	90.00	
Aubergine	1.20	0.90	0.20	12.00	26.00	10.00	
Avocado		2.20	1.50	17.00	10.00	42.00	290.00
Beet greens	2.20	1.30	3.00	119.00	40.00	6100.00	
Broccoli	3.60	1.50	0.30	103.00	78.00	2500.00	
Brussel sprouts	5.00	1.60	0.40	36.00	80.00	550.00	
Cabbage		1.30	0.80	0.20	49.00	29.00	130.00
Carrot	1.10	1.00	0.20	37.00	36.00	1100.00	
Cauliflower	2.70	1.00	0.20	25.00	56.00	60.00	
Celeriac	1.80	1.30	0.30	43.00	115.00	00.00	
Chicory greens	1.70	0.80	0.30	86.00	40.00	4000.00	
Cucumber	0.90	0.60	0.10	25.00	27.00	250.00	
Endive	1.70	0.90	0.10	81.00	54.00	3300.00	
Fennel	2.80	0.50	0.40	100.00	51.00	3500.00	
Lettuce	1.20	0.50	0.20	35.00	26.00	900.00	
Lettuce, romaine	1.30	0.70	0.30	68.00	25.00	300.00	
Lettuce, iceberg	0.90	0.50	0.10	20.00	22.00	1700.00	
Peas, green	6.30	2.00	0.50	26.00	120.00	640.00	
Peppers, sweet	1.20	1.40	0.22	9.00	22.00	420.00	
Sprouting beans	3.80	0.70	0.20	19.00	64.00	20.00	
Spinach	3.00	0.60	0.30	93.00	38.00	8100.00	
Tomato	1.10	0.50	0.20	13.00	00.27	900.00	
Turnip greens	3.00	0.80	0.90	246.00	58.00	7500.00	
Watercress	2.20	0.70	0.30	151.00	55.00	4900.00	

* Shown in mg

CALCIUM SUPPLEMENTS

Some forms of calcium are more easily absorbed or utilised than others and some in themselves contain high levels of phosphorous. The best forms are those which have a high calcium percentage (Ca) and a low percentage of phosphorous (P). The approximate average Ca:P ratios of some commonly available additives are given below. From this it will be noted that calcium carbonate is a very good additive whilst calcium phosphate is a comparatively poor source.

	% Ca	% P
Calcium borogluconate	8.50	00.00
Calcium carbonate	40.00	00.00
Calcium gluconate	9.25	00.00
Calcium lactate	18.00	00.00
Calcium phosphate - monobasic	17.00	26.00
Calcium phosphate - dibasic	30.00	23.00
Calcium phosphate - tribasic	39.00	20.00
Standard bone meal	30.00	15.00

in the diet can cause liver disorders, kidney problems, and can also affect the calcium metabolism. Excessive protein levels will also cause very rapid growth; much faster than wild tortoises experience. This causes grossly distorted carapace scutes, (pyramiding), and very dark coloration due to excessively thick layers of keratin in the carapace scutes. Bones are also affected, becoming porous and weak in structure. Where dietary studies have been conducted on various species of tortoises inhabiting desert habitat, it has been noted that an average protein intake is usually 3 to 7 percent.

Excessive fat should also be avoided. In studies on various types of desert dwelling tortoises, excessive fat has been found to accumulate in the body cavity, and also in the liver causing jaundice. Jaundice is caused by malfunction or damage to the liver. Therefore, in the author's opinion, feeding your sulcata (adults or hatchlings) a good variety of the natural foods listed will provide enough protein and fat without using dog food, meat, or other man- made tortoise foods.

FRUIT

As with commercial produce, fruit should be offered to your sulcata very sparingly. Too much fruit can cause high levels of sugar which can lead to intestinal problems. All fruit should be pitted and seeded before offering it to your tortoise, with the exception of melon seeds. Seeds and pits can be toxic and can get lodged in the throat. All fruits should be washed thoroughly. Pesticides and fertilizers are used on fruits and can be eaten by your tortoise, especially in the case of fruits that need to be peeled such as bananas.

VITAMINS AND CALCIUM

It is the author's opinion that even with a well-balanced varied diet it is still important to supplement with vitamins and calcium carbonate once a week, and especially so with hatchlings and breeding females. The sulcata is a very large tortoise, therefore they grow naturally at a fairly quick rate, making it even more important that their diet is supplemented with calcium carbonate and a good quality multi-vitamin compound with D3 and other essential minerals. This allows for proper development of their bones. For breeding females it helps with the production of eggs. Calcium carbonate is phosphorous free making it the best choice for a calcium supplement. It is available at most feed supply stores and is very inexpensive. Our choice for vitamins are Super Preen powder made by Blairs or Herptivite made by REP-CAL. This latter company also makes a very good pure calcium carbonate with vitamin D3 supplement. In Europe, Nutrobal is a readily available equivalent. Extra minerals can also be provided by means of a trace mineral block, which can be purchased at feed stores. The mineral block can be broken up into a powder and sprinkled on the food once a week, or the entire block can be placed in the enclosure for the tortoises to nibble on.

FERTILIZERS AND PESTICIDES

No fertilizers or pesticides should be used in or around any tortoise enclosures. This can have drastic consequences, poisoning your animals.

WATER

This is a controversial subject when it comes to sulcatas. Taking into consideration the sulcatas habitat which is very dry and the foods eaten in the wild, which are primarily dry grasses, it is hard to say how much water a sulcata needs. Our adult tortoises are offered water once a week during the summer months, and twice a month during winter. Hatchlings are offered water every other day during summer months and twice a week during winter. New research is being carried out at an increasing rate, so the water requirements of tortoises may be better understood in the near future.

It should be said that the diet recommended here is based on studies of other desert dwelling species, mainly North American Desert tortoises and some varieties of Mediterranean tortoises. We are not aware of any in-depth research concerning dietary specifics on Sulcatas. Although we have had good success in maintaining and breeding sulcatas following these dietary guidelines, we are not implying that this is the only way to successfully maintain and breed this species. Many other people have had good results and their methods concerning maintenance, diet and breeding should be also carefully considered. There are also other books available, written by successful tortoise breeders, that may offer other successful methods concerning the proper care and maintenance of tortoises. There are also, sadly, a number of books on the market which contain seriously inaccurate and in some cases even dangerous advice. One of the best things you can do is to join a reputable tortoise society. Other members are always willing to share advice, experiences and knowledge. You will soon discover which advice can be relied upon and which should be disregarded.

A fully grown adult. Note extended gular region. Geochelone sulcata is the largest continental land tortoise, surpassed in size only by the giant island species of the Galapagos and Seychelles

Male (left) and female (right) adult Geochelone sulcata

A large-scale sulcata egg incubator. Vermiculite substrate

The moment of hatching

A few weeks old

Geochelone sulcata is famous for its excavating skills

Sulcatas are also enthusiatic browsers

Care and Breeding of the African Spurred Tortoise

HOW TO SEX SPURRED TORTOISES

Accurate sexing of the Spurred tortoise is usually an easy task as long as the animal is at least 12 inches in length - tortoises smaller than this are, to say the least, very difficult. Any tortoise smaller than 12 inches would be at best a guess. Tortoises 12 inches or larger begin to show physical differences. Females will have a flat plastron, a very short tail, and small gular scutes. Males have a concave plastron, a much longer tail, and large forked gular scutes. The anal scutes of the male are generally very wide (and thicker) in comparison to the female anal scutes which are much narrower, forming a circular opening between the supracaudal shield and the anal scutes.

The male's tail is quite long so it is carried folded over to one side. The female's tail is very short and even when folded over, is scarcely a inch long, whilst that of the male is commonly 2 inches in length or longer.

The gular scutes of males are used for competing for territory and for fighting over females. They are very pronounced, and have a wide forked appearance as well as being much longer and heavier built. Female gulars are usually shorter, slightly forked, and are thinner built.

Males at about 14 to 15 inches in straight length are becoming sexually mature and will begin to show aggressive behavior towards other tortoises in their enclosure, ramming and mounting other tortoises in an attempt to establish territory and dominance. Usually this is not harmful to other tortoises of equal size but males can and do turn others over onto their backs. This is particularly dangerous in hot climates as sulcatas cannot right themselves very easily. Females largely ignore other tortoises and rarely show aggressive behavior (unless they are carrying eggs).

MEASURING THE TORTOISE

To accurately measure the length of your tortoise, turn the animal over onto its back and place a tape measure on the plastron measuring from the tip of the gular scutes to the supracaudal shield. This is the correct way to determine the length of the tortoise. The wrong way to determine length is to measure what is known as an over-the-curve measurement. This is done by measuring the tortoise over the carapace, so a 16 inch tortoise is usually at best a 14 inch animal. This is important when purchasing tortoises as size usually determines the price of the tortoise.

Typical combat using the gular as a battering ram and lever.

The correct way to measure a tortoise.

BREEDING *GEOCHELONE SULCATA*

Providing you have sexed your tortoises correctly and have both a male and a female, breeding is usually achieved with little effort. Keep in mind that they do need to be housed properly and furnished with egg laying sites. First your tortoise will have to be at least 15 inches in straight length. We have found that imported tortoises can and do breed, laying fertile eggs at 15 inches straight length. Our experience with captive born and raised sulcatas is that at the age of 11 years, and a length of at least 16 inches, breeding and egg laying will usually commence. Breeding season for our tortoises usually starts in July and extends into early November. The male will usually start by ramming the female with his gular scutes in an attempt to immobilize her. No biting has been observed with our tortoises. Once the female has been immobilized the male then mounts the female from the rear, his neck fully extended. His mouth is held open emitting a grunting sound. The back feet of the male are, presumably, used to stimulate the female in a hopping up and down motion scraping the marginal scutes of the female. The male also uses his tail to stimulate the female by stroking her cloacal area.

When the female is ready to mate she will raise the rear of her plastron up off the ground. When copulation begins she extends her front legs out to her sides and will remain in this position until copulation is completed. When mating is over the female usually leaves the area followed closely by the male. Mating may take place several times each season.

EGGS AND INCUBATION

After a successful copulation, gestation periods prior to nesting can be a minimum of 30 days, to as long as 90 days. The exact period seems to be more dependent on weather conditions than anything else. Our tortoises breed in late summer starting in July. If the weather stays warm they will lay their eggs usually without any problems. If the weather turns cold they seem to be very reluctant to lay until there are several days of sunny weather reaching 75 degrees or warmer. The female will then start pacing the enclosure sniffing the ground looking for a place to nest. This could take from one day to a couple of weeks. Once she has chosen the nest site and begins digging it can take from 2 to 6 hours to excavate the nest, lay her eggs, and finally cover the nest. When she has chosen a suitable spot she will start to dig with her front legs going in head first. After she has the hole about one foot deep she will turn around and start to dig out the chamber using her rear legs. When she is done digging out the egg chamber, she will usually rest for a few minutes and position herself directly over the egg chamber. She will soon start to lay her eggs, stopping to rest from time to time and arranging the eggs with her hind feet. This period is critical. Our own sulcatas have cracked and broken as many as 10 eggs during this arranging and burying proccess. It is usually best if you carefully take the eggs out of the nest while she is still laying them. You can sit quietly next to the female working your hand into the hole directly behind the tortoise. There is usually sufficient room. The eggs should be removed before she starts to arrange them, as this is when she is most likely to break them. If she cracks any eggs check to see if the thin membrane just inside the shell is broken. If it is, there is no hope for that particular egg. If the egg is cracked and the membrane is not broken, there is still hope. The author has had success using cloth Band-Aid. Cut the gauze middle out and discard, then clean the egg with a clean dry cloth or paper towel so that the Band-Aid will stick. Place the remaining ends of the Band-Aid over the entire crack. This must be done very delicately so as to not to further break the egg.

When removing the eggs from the nest do not disturb the female any more than necessary. Never attempt to take the female off the nest before she has finished laying her entire clutch. After the eggs are removed from the nest, they can be cleaned off with a clean dry cloth or paper towel and dated with a pencil (only) on the top. Then the eggs should be placed into the incubator. Care should be taken when removing eggs from the nest not to unnecessarily jar or roll them.

Geochelone sulcata can lay as many as 6 clutches of eggs per year. Clutches are usually laid 30 to 60 days apart depending on weather conditions. Clutch sizes range from 5 to 35 eggs

THE INCUBATOR

A very reliable and accurate thermometer and humidity gauge is the first requirement. There are many different types of incubators available. Most of them are designed for chicken eggs but some will work fine for tortoise eggs with a few modifications. Unlike bird eggs, tortoise eggs do not need circulating air fans. Tortoise egg shells are permeable to a certain degree unlike many reptile eggs, and, if subjected to fan forced circulating air, will usually dehydrate quickly. A complete lack of air circulation of the incubator should also be avoided. Still air can cause a lack of oxygen resulting in anoxia. Many of the small Styrofoam incubators without fans for chicken eggs work very well. There are small holes in the lid to allow for air circulation, but opening the lid on the incubator for about 30 seconds every day is recommended to allow for fresh air transfer. To modify the incubator just remove the wire mesh in the bottom and replace with dry vermiculite about 1 inch deep. It should also be mentioned that a good electronic proportional thermostat should be used instead of the mechanical types. Mechanical thermostats commonly fail due to the constant on off cycles required, and will usually fail at critical points of incubation. Proportional type thermostats do not cycle on and off but rather regulate the amount of electricity flow to the heating element. They are much more dependable and are very accurate. Once you have made the modifications plug the incubator in and let the temperature stabilize. Do not put the eggs in until your incubator has had a couple of days to stabilize. After the temperature has stabilized place a small dish of water inside the incubator. The dish of water is employed to help create local humidity within the incubator. Humidity does not seem to be critical in incubating *Geochelone sulcata* eggs, however. In our experience, humidity levels have been anywhere from as low as 20 percent to as high as 85 percent with no difference in hatching success. We are not aware of any studies on incubation humidity regarding sulcata eggs. Therefore it is our opinion that humidity levels should not be extremely low or high, but in the medium range of 40 to 60 percent. The temperature in the incubator is also variable from 82 degrees to 92 degrees. We have had equal success hatching sulcata eggs anywhere from 82 to 92 degrees with no visible effects to hatchlings. But as with humidity, we feel that somewhere in the medium range is best. Therefore, 86 to 88 degrees seems to work well. Incubation time is also variable. At 86 to 88 degrees incubation takes about four months. Cooler temperatures will take longer, whereas warmer temperatures will speed up incubation times. It is also believed that incubation temperature influences the sex of any off-spring.

CANDLING EGGS

There is some controversy as to whether eggs should be candled to determine if they are fertile. Unless you are very familiar with the process, it is not recommended. The end result does not change, whether you candle your eggs or not. Candling just increases the chance of jarring or rolling the egg by accident.

If you are the type of person who has to give it a try, candling must be carried out with great caution. The eggs should be at least 60 days old before candling will reveal anything. Remove the egg from the incubator, making absolutely sure you do not roll or jar the egg. Using a powerful flashlight in total darkness, hold the egg still and move the light around the egg by shining it through the egg. If the egg is fertile you should be able to see the embryo and blood vessels. If the egg is infertile, the yolk is usually settled in the bottom of the egg and the egg appears clear.

HATCHING

When the baby tortoise is ready to hatch it will pierce the egg making a small hole in the shell with its egg tooth. Do not attempt to hatch the egg yourself. At this time the baby tortoise will often stay in its shell for 24 to 48 hours before it hatches out completely. Normally, after the hatchling has pierced the egg, it takes about three days before it can be removed from the incubator, provided the yolk sack is totally absorbed. Once the first egg has began to hatch, the other eggs in the clutch will soon begin hatching. Within about a week the entire clutch should be hatched. If there are a couple of eggs left just give it time. Be patient, never attempt to hatch the egg yourself. If you do you might find a baby with an excessively large yolk sack that in most cases will die. Before the hatchling is removed from the incubator make sure it has absorbed its yolk sack, if it has not, then it should be returned to the incubator until the yolk sack has been entirely absorbed. Once the hatchling is removed from the incubator, place it immediately into a shallow dish of warm water. The water should be just deep enough so the tortoise can comfortably hold its head out of the water. Let the hatchling soak for about five to ten minutes, and allow it to drink if it wishes to. Then place it into whatever you have set up for your nursery. Most hatchlings will usually start eating within a day or two after they have been removed from the incubator. They should be offered food daily, and should be offered water every other day. Continue to soak the hatchlings about three times a week until they are about six months old. By this time, the watering schedule will be the same as for adults.

DIET

The diet for hatchlings is identical to that of adults. Providing the hatchling with a large variety of food is very important. It is also essential to provide adequate levels of vitamins and minerals, such as calcium carbonate, and natural sunlight to promote the formation of vitamin D. The diet should consist of naturally grown foods that are **high in fiber** content and **low in protein & fat.**

The use of a phosphorous free calcium supplement such as calcium carbonate is also vitally important. It is our opinion that most foods fed to tortoises already contain adequate phosphorous and in order to achieve an applied calcium to phosphorous ratio of five or six to one the calcium supplement should be phosphorous free. Many grasses, vetches, clovers, and other foods listed here can be easily grown in your yard or indoors using artificial lights and provide a good base-line diet

INDOOR HOUSING

Sulcata hatchlings can be kept in many different kinds of enclosures including aquariums, show tanks plastic or wooden boxes. Always make sure that the hatchlings are kept safe from any predators you may have in your home - dogs in particular like chewing on young tortoises! This is why it is necessary to have a screen lid on whatever you choose for the hatchlings home. Recommended substrates are hay, non-medicated rabbit pellets, and dried alfalfa. It is best to avoid entirely any substrate that could be dangerous if ingested such as sand, pebbles, or outdoor carpets etc. All the recommended substrates work very well, are easily cleaned, and, if eaten, cause no harm to the tortoise.

HEATING AND LIGHTING

A heat lamp on top of the enclosure is the best way to warm the hatchlings. It is our opinion that light or non-light emitting heat sources from above are best for supplying the heat for your hatchlings, we do not use heat rocks or heat pads. Incandescent shop light fixtures available at your local hardware store work very well when placed on the screen top of your hatchling enclosure. The temperature should run at about 95 degrees in the basking area under the heat light and at about 85 degrees during the day in the rest of the enclosure. You will usually have to do a little experimenting with bulb wattage to obtain the desired temperature. A fluorescent light should also be provided to intensiify lighting in indoor enclosures, as the heat light will not provide the tortoises with enough light. Hatchlings become inactive and lethargic if kept in lighting conditions which are not bright enough. It has been the author's experience that using full spectrum lights advertised for reptiles has little or no effect in providing beneficial ultra violet lighting. **There is no substitute for natural sunlight.** Hatchlings that are offered natural unfiltered sunlight in outdoor enclosures are much healthier in comparison to those housed indoors in artificial lighting. In areas where climate conditions will not allow the hatchlings to be put outdoors for long periods during winter weather, they can be placed in areas in your house were sunlight enters through an open window. Glass and plastics filter out any beneficial effects from natural sunlight. If the tortoises can be put outside even for just a couple of hours it is very beneficial. When hatchlings are kept indoors heat lamps and florescent lights should be turned on every morning and turned off at night in keeping with your seasonal photo period. Night-time temperatures should not normally drop below 65 degrees. A non light emitting heat source such as Pearlco © ceramic heat bulbs should be used if temperatures threaten to drop below 65 degrees at night.

OUTDOOR HOUSING

Housing hatchlings outdoors is recommended, provided that the weather in your locality permits this. With the sulcata, there are some very basic guide lines to stick to as far as an outside enclosure is concerned. The hatchlings must be kept in something that is completely safe from predators and which has no escape holes. Tortoises are excellent at both climbing and digging, so enclosure security is important. They should also have a shaded area to get out of the sun. Several types of grasses, vetches, and clovers should be grown in the outdoor enclosure to give the hatchlings grazing foods. Never put any tortoise outside in the sun using an aquarium as temperatures can reach lethal levels very quickly. The hatchlings also need to be checked frequently because they can flip over on their back very easily. Hatchlings should only be put in outdoor enclosures when weather permits and when they can be monitored closely.

CLEANING

Sanitary conditions are very important in keeping your sulcata healthy. Feces and uneaten food should be cleaned up on a daily basis. Substrates should be changed often and the tank should be cleaned out with a warm solution of water and just a few drops of bleach, then rinsed out and dried with a clean towel. Any dishes used to soak the hatchlings should not be reused until they have been thoroughly cleaned. The same applies to any dishes that may be used for food. Paper plates can be used as an alternative to having to wash food dishes every day.

KEEPING HATCHLINGS CLEAN

When needed, the sulcata can be bathed in warm running water (without soap) and gently cleansedwith a soft bristle brush to remove anything that has gotten into the grooves of its shell. Care must be taken not to brush in the vicinity of the tortoise's eyes. Usually, the best time to bathe the tortoise is just after it has been soaked. This will have loosened concreted dirt that has dried onto the shell. It is not necessary, nor is it recommended, to put any kind of oil on the shell to enhance carapace coloration. Oils will clog pores in the carapace, will encourage dirt to stick to the shell, and can interfere with thermoregulation.

VETERINARY PROBLEMS

> FINDING A QUALIFIED VETERINARIAN IN YOUR AREA SHOULD BE YOUR FIRST STEP IN KEEPING AND MAINTAINING TORTOISES. YOUR LOCAL HERP CLUB IS USUALLY THE BEST PLACE TO FIND A GOOD VETERINARIAN.

PARASITES

Parasites, if left untreated, can have dangerous effects on sulcatas. There are several types of common internal parasites that may be encountered.

NEMATODES

Round worms: (Ascarids) These worms are white, resembling spaghetti, and can range in size from 1/2 inch to as much 6 inches. These worms are very common. In mild cases the symptoms include anorexia and diarrhea, in severe cases stools will have visible worms, or the tortoise may vomit worms. Treatment consists of using Panacur © (fenbendazole). The dosage rate is usually 25 mg to 50 mg per kilo of the tortoise's weight repeated at 14 day intervals for two or three treatments. Treatment is given orally.

Pinworms: (Oxyurids) These are very small worms and are not usually seen by the naked eye. Symptoms typically include anorexia and diarrhea. Severe cases include perforations of the intestine and intestinal blockage. Treatment consist of Panacur © (fenbendazole) at 50 mg per kilo of tortoise weight repeated again in 14 days. Treatment is given orally.

FLAGELLATES

There are numerous species of flagellates organism, *Hexamita, Trichomonas*, etc. Flagellates can cause very serious problems in tortoises if not treated promptly. Symptoms include diarrhea, blood or mucous in stools, anorexia, dehydration, and the passage of undigested food. Treatment consist of Flagyl (metronidazole), given orally. There are several recommended dosing schedules ranging from 25 mg per kilo to 260 mg per kilo. The minimum dosage rate is given daily for 10 days, whilst the maximum dosage rate is usually given in the form of two treatments at 14 day intervals. Since dose rate and frequency may vary depending upon the levels and type of infection, consult your veterinarian.

HEXAMITIASIS

This is a very serious infection caused by *hexamita parva* and should be treated immediately. Symptoms are strongly smelling urine which may be tinged green and flecked with blood. Treatment is with Flagyl (metronidazole) at 50 mg per kilo for ten days. Also recommended is 260 mg per kilo in two treatments 14 days apart.

EXTERNAL PARASITES

These are usually ticks or mites, both of which are not very common with captive tortoises, but are occasionally encountered with wild caught animals. Fortunately, they are easily removed. A tick can be removed with either tweezers or fingers and then gently pulling until it is removed, including the head, then treating the area with Betadine ©.

Mites are most safely eradicated using a pyrethroid mite spray. Pyrethroids are a safer and more effective form of natural pyrethrum. Consult a specialist reptile veterinarian for application guidelines.

INJURIES

Skin injuries should be cleaned thoroughly with antiseptic. Apply a good topical antibiotic, and cover so flies cannot get to the wound. Most wounds will usually heal without any further problems.

Cracked or broken shells, or open wounds on carapace or plastron, should be cleaned thoroughly with antiseptic and taken to your vet for treatment and further repairs.

BACTERIAL INFECTIONS

RUNNY NOSE

This condition is typically caused by a bacterial infection (e.g., *Klebsiella* or *Pseudomonas*) or by mycoplasma organisms. Runny noses are often associated with maintenance at incorrect temperatures or with poor hygiene. Labored breathing, wheezing, discharge from the nose, or excessive mucous around the mouth are usually the first signs of a respiratory infection and must be treated as soon as possible. There are many drugs and dosage schedules depending on how severe the case is. Some commonly used drugs are Oxytetracycline, Ampicillin, and Baytril ©. The dosage schedule can range from 5 to 10 consecutive days. The drugs listed here are given by intramuscular injection.

This list is just a few of the more commonly encountered problems in captive sulcatas. Because of the similarity with symptoms, the complexity of drugs used to treat these problems, and other effects drugs may have on tortoises we can not over emphasize the point that a qualified veterinarian be located through your local herp club. Although a few drug types and dosages are listed always consult your veterinarian for diagnosis and proper drug administration.

A major contributing factor to disease problems in captive collections are diet, temperature, and fecal contamination of food and water. Overcrowding and introducing contagious animals into collections also account for many outbreaks. Neglect in any of these areas is sure to cause repeated parasitic and bacterial problems

STOMATITIS (MOUTH ROT)

Mouth rot is characterized by a sore-looking mouth, often with yellow, cheesy deposits. The bacteria which cause it are often resistant to treatment. Veterinary diagnosis and appropriate antibiotic therapy is essential. Most cases are treated by a combination of antibiotic injections with additional antibiotics applied directly to the mouth.

ULCERATIVE SHELL DISEASE (SHELL ROT)

This unpleasant condition can be initiated by minor shell injuries, and is also associated with unhygienic conditions. It may manifest as loose scutes, or as a foul smelling discharge from the shell. Minor cases may respond to regular daily cleaning with Betadine ©, and removal of all loose or infected tissue. Serious cases will require antiobiotic therapy. This condition is contagious, so isolate any affected animal at once.

EYE INFECTIONS

Swollen eyes may be caused by acute vitamin-A deficiencies, but are more usually associated with bacterial infections. Consult your vet as an accurate diagnosis is essential.

Further details of up-to-date treatment methods for tortoises may be found in the Practical Encyclopedia of Keeping and Breeding Tortoises and Freshwater Turtles by A. C. Highfield (Carapace Press, 1996) or in Reptile Medicine and Surgery by D. R. Mader (W. B. Saunders Company, 1996). Both books also contain a wealth of information on nutritional management and disease prevention.

Enjoying a drink from a garden hose.

Rear view of *Geochelone sulcata* with 'spur' visible on right. This tortoise also has a drilled supracaudal, probably for tethering when captured in Africa. This practice is both dangerous and painful.

FREQUENTLY ASKED QUESTIONS

WHY DOES MY SULCATA PACE THE CHAINLINK FENCE ?
Because it can see through it. Generally, if tortoises can see through fencing, they seem to be constantly unsettled. We do not recommend that the enclosure be made of anything your tortoise can see through. Also, because *Geochelone sulcata* are so strong, they will usually just push their way under any kind of wire fencing and escape. Tortoises can also seriously injure themselves on wire by getting cut or trapped.

HOW MUCH ROOM DOES EACH SULCATA NEED IN ITS PEN?
For hatchlings housed indoors, a ten or twenty gallon aquarium is usually large enough. A four inch tortoise will need at least a 55 gallon size aquarium. Hatchlings housed outdoors must be kept in pens that are escape and predator proof, with plenty of floor space Out door pens should be as large as possible to accommodate the tortoise, a house for the tortoise, and plenty of natural growing foods. When building the pen keep in mind how big you tortoise is capable of getting.

HOW MUCH ROOM DOES A SULCATA NEED IN ITS OUTDOOR BOX ?
The box needs to be big enough that when he walks in he should clear the door way by 8 inches to a foot. The floor space should be at least 4 times the size of your tortoise.

HOW MANY INCHES DO SULCATAS GROW IN A YEAR?
That answer depends on the age and diet of the tortoise. They will usually grow about 2 inches a year.

HOW BIG DO THEY GET ?
180 to 200 lbs., 30 to 36 inches long. Males are usually larger than females as adults.

HOW LONG DO THEY LIVE ?
Depending on the diet and the care given to your sulcata, it may live well over 100 years. Although we are not aware of any research on sulcata life expectancy, other types of giant tortoises can live 100 and very possibly 200 years.

CAN *GEOCHELONE SULCATA* HANDLE HUMIDITY ?
We are not aware of any scientific study on this topic, although they come from a dry arid climate they seem to do well in Florida and other states where the humidity levels are commonly 75 to 85 percent.

DOES *GEOCHELONE SULCATA* DIG ?

Yes, but generally, this will only happen if they are not adequately housed. If the housing is too small they will certainly tend to dig a lot. If the tortoise is provided with enough space, and adequate shade for the summer months, it will lessen the chances of your yard being rearranged. We have 8 large sulcatas in our personal group and no holes in the ground.

CAN YOU STOP THEM FROM DIGGING ?

Yes. As soon as digging is observed simply fill the hole in. If the tortoise goes back and digs it out again fill in the hole, then cover the hole with a piece of plywood and leave it there until the tortoise no longer is interested in that area. This may take as long as a couple of weeks. Just remember that females start their nest with their front legs, so don't be too quick to pull a female off a hole until you are sure whether or not she is digging a burrow or a nesting site.

DOES *GEOCHELONE SULCATA* HIBERNATE ?

No, that is why it is important that you provide your sulcata with a heated box for the winter.

SHOULD I PUT A POND OR WATER FALL IN THEIR ENCLOSURE FOR THEM TO SOAK IN ?

No, the sulcata is a essentially desert tortoise from Africa. It is important to keep their enclosure dry. Standing water of any kind should be avoided. It is very difficult to keep clean and also provides a breeding ground for unwanted pathogens.

IS IT SAFE TO KEEP MY SULCATA IN CLOSE CONTACT WITH WITH OTHER SPECIES OF TORTOISES ?

NO! All tortoise species should be housed and maintained separately. Viral and bacterial problems will almost always cause devastating affects on mixed tortoise groups. Behavior problems will also be encountered. Some tortoises are very shy and others, as in the case of the *Geochelone sulcata*, can be very bold, intimidating, and highly aggressive at times.

WHY IS THERE A HOLE DRILLED IN THE BACK OF HIS SHELL ?

If your sulcata has a hole drilled in the back of its shell there is a very good chance that your tortoise is an import. The hole is drilled into the supracaudal shield and was presumably used to tether the animal to a post to keep it from escaping after capture This was certainly a painful procedure for the animal, and the practice is to be condemned.

IS IT SAFE TO PAINT MY SULCATA'S SHELL WITH A NON-TOXIC PAINT?

No. Paint on any tortoises shell is damaging to the animal and can seriously interfere with thermoregulation.

WHERE DO FEMALES LAY THEIR EGGS ?

In most cases they lay their eggs on the perimeter of the pen, but on occasion they might lay their eggs under a bush or in their heated box.

WHY NOT JUST LEAVE THE EGGS IN THE GROUND ?

There are a couple of things to consider if you are thinking about leaving the eggs in the nest to hatch naturally. First is the weather, can they be flooded when it rains? Secondly, temperatures may be far too hot or, more likely, too cold. Females will often use the same nest site many times and if the previous nest is still full of eggs there is a good chance she will dig them up, destroying them. We have also had predatory insects get into nests and destroy all the eggs. It is always much safer to put eggs in an incubator where they can be monitored carefully.

DO SULCATAS BITE ?

No. *Geochelone sulcata* is very docile towards people and rarely if ever shows any aggressive behavior towards humans. They will readily take food out of your fingers being careful not to bite. Although brightly colored fingernails or toenails will sometimes demand a closer look and maybe even a little taste.

WILL A SULCATA DIE IF TURNED ON ITS BACK ?

If turned over onto its back in the sun your tortoise can become overheated very quickly and die. This can occur in a frighteningly short space of time. Even out of the sun, internal damage can occur, such as gut torsions and respiratory arrest.

AGGRESSIVE BEHAVIOR: SHOULD THEY BE SEPARATED ?

By separating the tortoises you are merely prolonging the inevitable. This is a matter of establishing territory and dominance. A watch full eye should be kept on them to make sure the female is not flipped over on her back, and she should be checked frequently for injuries. This behavior is usually encountered when new tortoises are added to an existing group. Given time, they will work out dominance and territory conflicts on their own without any further problems. Males, in some cases, may not be housed together without conflict unless provided very large areas.

DO TORTOISES GET VITAMINS FROM NATURAL SUN LIGHT ?

Yes, one of the most important of all vitamins to tortoises is vitamin D3, which aids in the absorption of calcium. It is produced by the action of natural sunlight on the tortoise's skin. It can (and should) also be provided orally, by means of a balanced calcium-D3 supplement.

WHAT ABOUT DOGS AND TORTOISES?

It is our opinion that dogs should not be kept with tortoises as they can cause injury even if just playing. Tortoises can get chewed up, carried off, and even eaten by the dog that in other ways wouldn't hurt a fly. I have had many calls from people that had a dog that either chewed up or killed their tortoise, but prior to this the dog never had hurt anything. Dog feces are also readily consumed by tortoises and tortoises feces seem to be irresistible to most dogs. This is not a recommended part of the diet for either animal and should be avoided!

HOW WARM SHOULD THE OUTDOOR BOX BE KEPT IN THE WINTER

During cold weather it is our opinion that the tortoises outdoor box should be allowed to cool down to 60 to 65 degrees overnight. This allows a natural cooling period much the same as they would experience in the wild. Daytime temperatures should be maintained at 80 to 95 degrees.

BIBLIOGRAPHY & SUGGESTED READING

Keeping and Breeding Tortoises in Captivity - by A.C. Highfield, published 1990 by Carapace Press, London, UK.

Care & Maintenance of the Leopard Tortoise *Geochelone pardalis* - by A.C. Highfield and Jill Martin, published 1990 by Tortoise Trust.

Understanding Reptile Parasites - by Roger J. Klingenberg D.V.M. Published 1993 by the Herpetocultural Library.

Proper Nutrition for Grazing Tortoises - by Dr Ross Prezant, published in Vol.XI/No.6 of the Nov/Dec 1995 Newsletter for the National turtle and Tortoise Society.

Practical Encyclopedia of Keeping and Breeding Tortoises & Freshwater Turtles - by A.C. Highfield, published 1996 by Carapace Press London, UK.

Tortoise Trust Guide to Tortoises & Turtles - by A.C. Highfield, published 1994 by Carapace Press, London, UK

Nutritive Quality and Mineral Content of Potential Desert Tortoise Foods - by E. Durant McArthur, Stewart C. Sanderson, and Bruce L. Webb. Published in a research paper by the United States Department of Agriculture at Forest Service Intermountain Research Station. nd.

Veterinary Management of Tortoises and Turtles - by Stuart McArthur M.R.C.V.S. Published 1996 by Blackwell Science, Oxford, UK

Turtles of the World - by Carl H. Ernst and Roger W. Barbour, published 1989 by the Smithsonian Institution.

CARAPACE PRESS
New for Sulcata keepers!

Practical Care of Leopard and Sulcata Tortoises

Detailed VHS 'How-To' Video complete with a comprehensive and expertly written book for only $19.95

For full details visit our web site and on-line store at

http://www.vidi-herp.com

Many more titles available for tortoise, turtle, gecko, snake and frog keepers!

The Tortoise Trust

For the Conservation and Captive Welfare of Tortoises & Turtles

Regular Newsletter - Specialist help and advice

http://www.tortoisetrust.org